100

Questions
For The
Soul

ifie natasha

for the soul.

Soul

/sōl/

noun.

the place
where life,
identity, feeling,
thought, and
action reside.

Ask yourself these questions everyday. Once a week. Twice a month. And every moment you need to remember who you are, what you need, or where you're going. Quiet your mind and listen. **Your soul has the answers.**

IFIE NATASHA

one.

If today was a perfect day, how would you spend it?

two.

Ask yourself, does it have to be this way?

three.

What are you looking for?

four.

What situation do you find yourself in over and over?

five.

When was the last time you tried something different?

six.

Are you going after who you are or what you want?

seven.

What are you ignoring?

eight.

What finished works have you abandoned?

nine.

What is life teaching you right now?

ten.

What are you doing because you feel obligated?

eleven.

Who are you trying to impress?

twelve.

What have you accomplished this year?

thirteen.

What do you have control over?

fourteen.

How did you love yourself today?

fifteen.

What haven't you done in a while that you'd like to get back to doing?

sixteen.

What makes you smile?

seventeen.

What does freedom feel like?

eighteen.

What's the most freeing thing you've ever done?

nineteen.

When is the last time you've done something that freeing?

twenty.

Whose rules are you following?

twenty one.

What has this year shown you?

twenty two.

What would you call this year if you could give it a name?

twenty three.

What's the word for next year?

twenty four.

What joy are you denying yourself?

twenty five.

What lies are you telling yourself?

twenty six.

When was the last time you told yourself yes?

twenty seven.

What gives you peace?

twenty eight.

What are you afraid of?

twenty nine.

Are you truly living?

thirty.

When was the last time you complimented yourself?

thirty one.

Are you living your dream life?

thirty two.

What are you currently feeding your soul?

thirty three.

How did you feed your spirit today?

thirty four.

If you were a child, what would you spend your day doing?

thirty five.

Are you afraid to be alone?

thirty six.

When was the last time you said "I could do this for the rest of my life?"

thirty seven.

When do you feel most alive?

thirty eight.

When was the last time you took a deep breath?

thirty nine.

What do you love most about yourself?

forty.

Who are you becoming?

forty one.

Do you love who you are becoming?

forty two.

Are you willing to give up everything you have, in order to get everything you want?

forty three.

What was the last goal you accomplished?

forty four.

Is there anything in your life that you need to let go of?

forty five.

Who are you trying to prove yourself to?

forty six.

How do you respond to pain?

forty seven.

What was beautiful about today?

forty eight.

What heals you?

forty nine.

When was the last time you got your heart broken?

fifty.

Are you letting guilt guide you in any area of your life?

fifty one.

Have you connected with yourself today?

fifty two.

Are you happy?

fifty three.

What is God saying through you today?

fifty four.

Are you living from a place of pain or identity?

fifty five.

When was the last time you did something you thought you couldn't do?

fifty six.

What are you chasing ?

fifty seven.

What are you certain of?

fifty eight.

How is your relationship with yourself?

fifty nine.

Is there something in your life you should stop doing?

sixty.

What do you want?

sixty one.

What are you
carrying
that doesn't
belong to you?

sixty two.

What is your greatest accomplishment?

sixty three.

What is your greatest triumph?

sixty four.

What is your greatest failure?

sixty five.

What has been your greatest lesson in life?

sixty six.

What do you see when you look in the mirror?

sixty seven.

What do you need?

sixty eight.

What do you have?

sixty nine.

How will you feed your spirit today?

seventy.

What does your name mean?

seventy one.

What are you most proud of?

seventy two.

What secrets are you holding on to?

seventy three.

When do you feel most like yourself?

seventy four.

What was your favorite thing to do when you were young?

seventy five.

What makes you happy?

seventy six.

What makes you sad?

seventy seven.

What makes you angry?

seventy eight.

What would you change about your life?

seventy nine.

What do you fantasize about?

eighty.

What makes you cry?

eighty one.

What makes you laugh really, really, hard?

eighty two.

How are you feeling today?

eighty three.

What is your earliest memory of love?

eighty four.

What have you been meaning to do that you haven't done yet?

eighty five.

What simple things do you enjoy most?

eighty six.

What do you spend money on without regret?

eighty seven.

Where does your beauty lie?

eighty eight.

What is your best quality?

eighty nine.

What is your biggest weakness?

ninety.

What do you want today to feel like?

ninety one.

If you could eliminate one thing from your life right now, what would it be?

ninety two.

When was the last time you felt free?

ninety three.

What has been your greatest lesson this week?

ninety four.

What are you seeking?

ninety five.

What do you need to change?

ninety six.

What do you want more than anything?

ninety seven.

What should you stop doing?

ninety eight.

What should you start doing?

ninety nine.

What dream have you forgotten about?

one hundred.

If you could do anything in the world, for the rest of your life, what would you do?

ASK QUESTIONS,
YOU'LL FIND ANSWERS...

Made in the USA
Columbia, SC
01 November 2020